DAD WAS A CARPENTER

DAD WAS A CARPENTER

*A Father, a Son, and the Blueprints
for a Meaningful Life*

KENNY KEMP

HarperSanFrancisco
A Division of HarperCollins*Publishers*

DAD WAS A CARPENTER: *A Father, a Son, and the Blueprints for a Meaningful Life*. Copyright © 2001 by Kenny Kemp. All rights reserved. Printed in the United States of America. No part of this book may be used or reproduced in any manner whatsoever without written permission except in the case of brief quotations embodied in critical articles and reviews. For information address HarperCollins Publishers Inc., 10 East 53rd Street, New York, NY 10022.

HarperCollins books may be purchased for educational, business, or sales promotional use. For information please write: Special Markets Department, HarperCollins Publishers Inc., 10 East 53rd Street, New York, NY 10022.

HarperCollins Web site: http://www.harpercollins.com
HarperCollins®, ♛®, and HarperSanFrancisco™ are trademarks of HarperCollins Publishers Inc.

FIRST EDITION
Designed by Joseph Rutt
Art by Kathleen Edwards

Library of Congress Cataloging-in-Publication Data
Kemp, Kenny.
Dad was a carpenter : blue prints for a meaningful life /
Kenny Kemp.—1st ed.
p. cm.
ISBN 0–06–251763–5 (cloth: alk paper)
1. Kemp, O. C. 2. Kemp, Kenny. 3. Fathers—Biography.
4. Fathers and sons—Case studies. I. Title.
HQ 756 .K395 2001
306.874'2'092—dc21
00–054096

01 02 03 04 05 ❖/RRD(H) 10 9 8 7 6 5 4 3 2 1

To Joy, who shares my love of words,
and Bonnie, who shares my love of art,
thank you for helping me nail this together.

My warmest thanks also to
Joe Durepos, agent and good friend,
and to my editor Gideon Weil,
who is too young to be so wise.

K. K.

CONTENTS

CHAPTER ONE

Blueprint

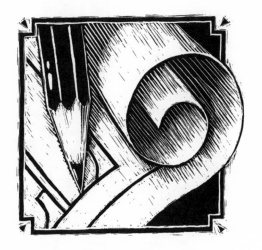

Watch it when you make a deal with God—be sure to keep your end of the bargain.

I lied. Dad was not really a carpenter. He didn't work in the trades at all. He was a pharmacist—an ordinary man with poor eyesight, gapped teeth, and no hearing in one ear, who struggled through high school, then flight school, then college, where Mom helped him with his trig homework.

By the time we became acquainted, Dad was a pharmacist at Grossmont Hospital in La Mesa, a San Diego suburb. When we'd visit him at work, there were always lots of interesting toys in his office—little goodies that drug salesmen would hand out (back in the days when the term *drug salesman* didn't have such an ominous undertone): pads of notepaper with the name of some new medication emblazoned on them in red italics, a huge two-toned capsule inscribed with the words *Chlor-Trimeton,* and pencils and rulers and so on, fascinating things for any five-year-old. I still have some of those goodies, and when

3

I visit my mom I always notice that she has drawers full of them—dusty archaeological finds, faded in memory.

Mom's tendency to keep *everything* has always been both a comfort and a consternation to me. She has enough white plastic Cool Whip containers to keep every leftover in southern California fresh. *Readers' Digests* from the late forties. Butterick dress patterns from the sixties. The memories in Mom's house abound—most of them as warm and tasty as her butterflake rolls.

But there are some memories in that house I don't want, and as I was driving south on Interstate 5 that day before Christmas, I knew this was a day I'd always remember—for good or bad. I hoped it would be a good memory, but I'm a realist. Today would be hard.

My father was dead.

CHAPTER TWO

Paintbrush

Patch everything up—especially your relationships.

I came to San Diego with the express purpose of cleaning out Dad's garage and spending Christmas with Mom, her first as a widow. I am the fourth of seven children—five girls and two boys. I'm the middle child, but I don't exhibit any of the typical attributes: the pleaser, the peacemaker, the forgotten soul. I'm Type A from B to Z, probably an attempt to distinguish myself from the crowd (as if being a boy amid five girls wasn't distinction enough). My brother Virl, the oldest, always seemed above the fray that I found myself in. Today, he would be helping me help Mom begin the grieving process.

Dad had died four months earlier in the sweltering humidity of a San Diego August, and we now felt it was time. His clothes still hung in the closet, the walls of his den were still papered with photos of airplanes, and Mom was still catching herself calling out to him to bring in a can of cling peaches from the pantry.

We're doing this for her, I told myself as I pulled into the driveway.

I believed it, too.

Dad's garage was an amazing sight—by far the most interesting aspect of the home. Several years ago my sister Bonnie painted Dad's favorite landscape on the garage door. It was the Grand Tetons as seen from the east, across Teton Lake. Bonnie thought he'd like it there. He did; the neighbors did not. But, notwithstanding the comments they made about the "appropriateness" of a garage door painting, Bonnie went ahead, with Dad's blessing.

It wasn't the first time our family had foisted garage door art upon innocent bystanders. Thirty years ago Dad's mother, Bea, painted a wildlife scene on *her* garage door. I was ten then, and it was my introduction to Art with a capital *A*.

A swift, crashing stream burst over rapids and exposed rock, slicing a quicksilver path between dense evergreens that hugged the steep banks. In the distance craggy peaks split an icy blue sky. On an exposed rock in midstream two giant brown bears swiped at each other, their teeth flashing. To one side, a silver trout lay forgotten, the object of the duel. That scene will always define how I look at nature, not as a quiet pastoral meditation but as a staging ground for deadly conflict.

Grandma's neighbors disliked the scene at first but were eventually won over by the utter brazenness of a painting eight feet tall by fifteen feet wide. Grandma was an amateur, but her aspirations were grandiose, at least in terms of size. The painting became a popular tourist destination. I never considered whether it was acceptable to paint a garage door that way or not. Dad always said it was her garage and she could do with it what she liked.

He must have believed it, too, because his garage was in the same tradition. With the Tetons gracing the door, you could bet there was something interesting going on inside. He was always in there, fixing or building something. And if you made the mistake of wandering by, he had a job waiting for you, whether steadying a socket wrench, holding the droplight as he lay under the car, or tightening a bolt.

I used to go over the back fence and through the neighbor's yard to avoid passing the garage, because Dad always had a chore in there with my name on it.

I turned off the ignition and got out of the car. The painting on the garage door was peeling a little, the disadvantage of acrylic paint in a humid climate and ten years of morning sun.

I slowly lifted the garage door and stepped inside to visit with my father.

CHAPTER THREE

Tape Measure

Building a go-cart with your son is better than taking him to the Indy 500.

When I was eight years old, go-carts were all the rage. Dad became a revered figure in the neighborhood when he built my brother and me a go-cart that was more than just an apple box nailed to a skateboard. Instead of using the traditional feet-steering method, Dad held up a flywheel from an old clothes dryer. "This gives me an idea!" he said, and we set to work.

The cart was shaped like an *I*, the main frame a sturdy two-by-ten about six feet long, with two-by-fours connected at the top and bottom, forming axles with hefty lawnmower wheels mounted on each end. The rear axle was nailed solidly to the frame, but the front pivoted for steering. A padded seat amidships gave easy access to the pivoting hand brake, which dragged on the ground, slowing the vehicle to a stop (hopefully) before impact.

All of this was pretty standard, except for the steering mechanism. Here's where Dad's ingenuity blossomed. Using a broomstick, a length of clothesline, and the flywheel, he engineered a design that guaranteed technical superiority over all other comers. He nailed the clothesline to the left end of the front axle near the wheel, brought it up and wound it around the broomstick (which was set at an angle to form a steering column), then headed it back down to the right end of the front axle near the opposite wheel. The flywheel was mounted on the raised broomstick end and became the steering wheel. We drove it like a real car. We turned the flywheel right, and, lo and behold, the go-cart went right as well.

As I stood by, watching him put the finishing touches on the cart, I was pleased but not amazed. After all, Dad rebuilt a Model A he found in a vacant lot near his house when he was only twelve. So when the neighborhood kids came by to see our state-of-the-art go-cart, Dad dismissed their oohs and aahs with a wave of the hand. "Just using what we had, is all," he said, and he turned back to the workbench where he was rigging up a radio to an old car battery so he could listen to KNXT news while he worked.

The go-cart was so vastly superior to the other neighborhood models that no one else even brought theirs out to play anymore. Instead, we treated the kids to rides in ours.

It's interesting: I cannot for the life of me remember Dad ever pushing my brother or me in that go-cart or standing on the sidewalk shouting encouragement as we raced down the street. What I do remember well was that I had the best go-cart in the world and that he'd built it for me. More than that didn't need saying—by either of us.

CHAPTER FOUR

Connections

Quality time is a myth—all time is
quality time.

When I turned twelve I became a Boy Scout. I had been an eager Cub and Webelo and was excited to enter young manhood. This, of course, meant hiking the famous John Muir Trail in California's High Sierra mountains.

Our troop planned to tackle one fifty-mile segment called the Twin Lakes, named for two crystalline lakes along the trail, high above the tree line, surrounded by nothing but an impossibly blue sky, craggy rocks, and lichen. "Like a lake on the moon," I was told, which ignited my imagination. I was an avid space buff who had clipped every article about the Mercury and Gemini space programs out of the newspaper. I was excited to see the lakes, but I was also afraid. I was small for my age, and no other Tenderfoot scouts in my troop were attempting the trek. I begged Dad to go with me, and he agreed, setting to work on what was, for him, the most exciting part: organizing our gear.

Of course, no store-bought pack would do for Dad—too expensive. Plus, they didn't have enough features, and *features* were what Dad was all about.

He built the frames from slender aluminum tubing, purchased bright yellow nontear nylon material, and Mom sewed the packs up according to Dad's specifications.

Finally, on a warm Saturday morning, we took a shakedown hike on nearby Black Mountain, a barren, rocky height whose pinnacle boasted a dozen radio antennae and a smoggy view of San Diego. At the summit, Dad pronounced our packs good and our blisters bad. He was interested in the former; I was concerned about the latter.

I have a picture of myself, most likely taken on one of the first days of the trek. I am standing on a dead-fall near a river, the yellow backpack towering over my head, my thumbs hooked into my belt, looking tired. As I look closer, I see another, deeper emotion: fear. I was terrified I wouldn't make it the whole

way. I was small, inexperienced, cold, and home-
sick.

I remember the second day of the trek, a Sunday.
Dad and I were straggling behind, due mostly to me.
It was nearing dark, and we still had a couple of miles
to go. Everyone else had already made it to camp. I
was beginning to feel the first twinges of fear that I
might not be able to hike all fifty miles with a forty-
pound pack on my back, but I was most afraid of
telling Dad this. I feared his response would be cryp-
tic and harsh: *Quit your bellyaching!*

I sat down on a rock to rest, the weight of the
pack and of my young life pressing down upon me.
Dad stood on the path, impatience in his eyes, saying
nothing. I looked up at him, saw his disappointment,
and felt hot tears building behind my eyes. I blinked
them back and looked away, ashamed to be such a cry-
baby, to disappoint my dad, who had never, in
twelve years of my life, disappointed me.

When I brushed an errant tear away and looked
up at him, he was looking at me. I was shocked to see
his eyes glistening with tears as well. He wordlessly

shucked his pack and helped me off with mine. He sat down next to me and looked down the trail where I was looking. For a long time we sat there, saying nothing.

"What time is it?" I asked finally.

Dad looked at his watch. "Seven-thirty."

"You know what they're doing at home right now?" I asked, confused at his tears and ashamed of my own.

He shook his head.

"They're probably eating ice cream and popcorn and watching *Walt Disney*." I looked up at him.

Dad smiled and nodded. "Maybe they're having Mom's milkshakes."

"Yeah," I ventured, "with chocolate syrup mixed in."

He put his arm around my shoulders and nodded again. We looked down the trail together in the gathering darkness. I rested my head against his chest and sighed. Maybe it would be all right. Maybe I'd make it through this after all.

CHAPTER FIVE

Saw

Never cut down a tree when you can
build around it.

W_e moved from the small suburb of Lemon Grove five miles across town to the equally small suburb of La Mesa the day after Christmas in 1968. Dad never let holidays get in the way of a project.

The move was, in many ways, a disappointment. Our new home was a step down. In our last place, Dad had built an incredible family room with a varnished, open-beamed ceiling and a colorful asphalt tile floor of his own design, which included a commanding, multihued *K* and a huge black, red, and green tile thunderbird. Around the room's perimeter ran a stair-stepped Mayan spiral motif, which always looked to me like the border was flexing its biceps. Beyond the sliding glass door Dad put in a swimming pool, cemented the entire backyard, and built a dollhouse for my sisters that was often mistaken for a guest house because of its size.

At the south end of the yard Dad built a patio, though not the flimsy, aluminum-roofed kind you most often see. This patio was built from the same materials as the family room: leftover glue-laminate beams and tongue-and-groove one-by-six planks salvaged from the construction of our church building. Dad was the unpaid construction manager, and his donated time carried at least one benefit: the right to purchase all leftover materials at a discount. Loath to cut down a large shade tree that stood where the patio would be built, Dad simply cut a hole in the roof. Not surprisingly, that patio stayed quite cool during the summer days.

When we got the news that we were moving, we kids were dumbfounded. How could we leave a home that Dad had just barely finished so perfectly, right down to the palms, elephant ears, and hibiscus plants surrounding the pool? There was no lawn in the backyard. (Since I was of lawnmowing age, the day we poured concrete was a red-letter day for me.) And, to further cement my love for him, Dad had nearly eradicated the lawn in the front yard as well. What we had was a huge pepper tree surrounded by an ivy garden, ringed in rock. In a crook of the front walk, Dad had planted a cactus and rock garden full of fascinating stones we had found on our vacations to the desert and Mexico.

Compared to the Eden we were leaving, our new house was on such a small lot that there was no room for even a patio, much less a pool and the grandmother of all dollhouses. It was poorly designed to boot, shaped like a U with the front door so far down the throat of the U that when you rang the bell you were only twenty feet from the back-yard. Looking back, I'm convinced the fact that the garages in both houses were identical in size was the real reason Dad bought this ungainly new home on the tiny lot.

He took apart the attic in the old garage, num-bered the joists and planks, and hauled them over to our new home. Mom had barely unpacked the dishes before Dad drafted the children to help him rebuild the attic in the new garage. Everything fit like a puzzle. The stenciled numbers my sister Gail painted on each piece of wood are still visible today.

As soon as it was completed, the attic filled up with boxes of Halloween costumes, camping equipment, school projects, and a two-year supply of cracked wheat. Once, in an attempt to prepare us for Armageddon, Mom and Dad made us eat the cracked wheat for breakfast. It had to be soaked overnight so it wouldn't chip our teeth. In the morning it was drained, drowned in milk, and buried in sugar. It still tasted like gravel. When we mutinied, even Dad had to admit that there were worse things than going hungry.

Along the south wall of the garage Dad built his workbench. As a hospital department head, he had access to what was thrown out when they remodeled. Over the years he managed to bring home countertops, chests of drawers, lamps, and electrical wiring.

In a nonstop burst of creativity one weekend, Dad built a chandelier from several cast-off patient-room lamps, each of which had a cone-shaped lampshade pointing upward from a round base and another long, bendable arm that ended in a shade pointing down for reading. Dad painstakingly bent a sheet of aluminum one foot wide by six feet long into the shape of a honeycomb cell and painted it black. He then attached a light fixture to each of the six faces, the long bendable arms pointing down like spindly black spider legs ending in cone-shaped feet.

The other lampshades pointed heavenward, lighting the vaulted ceiling far above. Inside the aluminum cell, he suspended glass vials filled with colored water. A floodlight shone down through them, glowing red, orange, and yellow, like some sort of fiery booster rocket.

Opinions as to its beauty varied, of course, but we all agreed on one thing: it would always be called the *lunar landing module*.

Like a great black spider hovering overhead, it was such a strange and marvelous invention that people invariably smiled when they saw it.

CHAPTER SIX

Glue

Memories are stubborn—they'll survive
even fires.

As I was walking home from school during my freshman year, a neighbor kid drove by yelling that my house was on fire. I laughed and waved him off, but, when I looked to the sky, I saw a plume of black smoke boiling up over my neighborhood. I ran home as fast as I could.

Our tax dollars were at work. Everybody was there. Firefighters had strung hoses from the end of the street, and two red pumpers were parked cock-eyed in front of the house, which was indeed on fire. Mom was running about, giving orders, and surprisingly, everyone—even the police and firemen—was taking them.

When the smoke cleared and the blackened water dried, we discovered a box of home movie film had been placed too close to the water heater in the garage and had ignited. Fortunately, the garage was connected to the house only by a breezeway, and structural damage was limited to the north wall of the garage and the roof. But the emotional damage was extensive. In Dad's jigsaw-puzzle attic my mother had kept all her photo albums, letters, and keepsakes, and much of it was reduced to soggy ashes.

I remember her crying, not over the damage to the garage or the simple embarrassment of setting one's own house on fire, but over the burned and ruined photos and home movies Dad had captured on his Super 8 camera, the same guilty film that had set the house afire.

Every Christmas, at the crack of dawn, we kids would line up in the hallway, from the youngest to the oldest, dressed in the new pajamas Mom had made. When Dad was ready with the camera, the door would open and in we'd march, braving the blinding bank of floodlights. We smiled and waved, feeling like stars at our own movie premiere. And I guess we were.

In later years he transferred the surviving films to video, placing all the Christmas movies in chronological order, starting with 1957. I have to laugh. Furnishings and gifts change from year to year, but the expressions on the kids' faces remain the same: tiny hands shield light-blinded eyes, eyelids are stuck together with sleep, bed-head hair sticks straight up—Christmas at the Kemps.

After the presents were opened, Dad would film each of us sitting proudly amid our holiday plunder, my parents' threats that *this* Christmas would not be as extravagant as last year buried under mounds of wrapping paper and shiny ribbon.

CHAPTER SEVEN

Bits (and Pieces)

If you break it, you fix it. Consequence is
the best teacher.

Two weeks after getting my driver's license, I was in an automobile wreck. I was turning left at an intersection and didn't see the car roaring over the rise from the opposite direction. The Mustang was totaled and its driver badly shaken up, but I was driving our two-tone green 1960 Dodge Sierra station wagon. I didn't get a scratch (Dad had installed seat belts long before Detroit included them as standard equipment), but the front end of the Dodge was badly mangled.

That Saturday, Dad and I went to a wrecking yard (I'm pretty sure *he* drove). There we found another Sierra with the front end intact. He supervised while I removed the grille, bumper, hood, fenders, and radiator. It was a very hot day, the dust was thick in the air, and I was soon covered with grease, dirt, and sweat. I paid the man $100 from my paper route earnings for the parts, and we took them home.

As we looked over the replacement parts strewn across the garage floor, I commented that this shouldn't take too long. Dad smiled and said I might be surprised. He said he'd be available for consultation but I was to perform the work myself. He turned and went inside. I stared after him, slack-jawed. I'd never be able to repair the car by myself. I knew it and he knew it. But there I was anyway, alone in the garage, with this impossible task ahead of me.

After the shock wore off, I ventured inside and found Dad sitting in his lounger, reading. "Dad," I said meekly, "you're kidding, right? You're gonna help me, aren't you?"

He never even looked up from his *National Geographic*. He just said, "Nope."

After a long moment, I turned and went back outside. I stood before the mangled monstrosity I'd created and cursed my father. I kicked the bumper, stomped around, and bored hateful stares through the wall that separated the garage from the living room.

Eventually defeat settled over me and I picked up a wrench, found a bolt that needed loosening, and began work.

It took me more than two months to fix the car. Dad would come out occasionally and offer advice, and a couple of times he even got under the car and helped. When he did, I was so thankful, so filled with gratitude, that I wanted to hug him and cry. But he'd crawl out, frown, hand me the wrench, and say something like, "It's right there, you just gotta use your eyes," and my heart would turn to glass. I'd want to punch him in his big stomach and yell at him, but I never did. I knew there would be a next time and I'd need his help again.

He treated everyone like that. He never did something for you just because you asked him to and he knew how. He seemed to know when you'd get more out of doing it yourself, even if it meant a poor job and the family car out of commission for two long months. I guess he knew the difference between giving a man a fish and teaching him how to bait a hook.

As I worked on the front end of the Dodge, as on so many other occasions, Dad was showing me how to cast a line out into life's river, even though I don't think he owned a fishing pole.

CHAPTER EIGHT

T Square

Don't send your kids to church—take them.

I was a troubled teenager. I turned fifteen in 1970, when the world was being turned upside down by Vietnam, drugs, and riots in the streets. My parents' generation had literally saved the world, and they did it by following orders and doing their duty. They trusted their parents and leaders and made incredible sacrifices.

And they were absolutely dumbfounded that their children seemed so disinclined to do the same.

My father, the oldest son of a disciplinarian, would brook no insurrection or sass. In all my life, I never talked back to him, fearful of his looming physical presence but even more afraid of his silent disapproval.

I grew up in a devout household. We attended church regularly, and I went willingly until I was about fifteen, when I began to question everything. I didn't know it at the time, but it was my solid grounding in faith and family that gave me license to ask the very questions my parents seemed unable to answer to my satisfaction. I guess I must've known on some level that there would always be a safe place to return to after my wanderings. And wander I did. Always an experimental sort, I liked to know things for myself, not just take them on someone else's word. This led to some difficult trials, to put it mildly.

The day before my eighteenth birthday, after a particularly bad argument with my mother, I moved out of my parents' house. I was certain that my parents were intent on preventing me from experiencing anything fun, exciting, or different. I moved in with a couple of high school friends near Balboa Park in downtown San Diego. At night, in the bed Dad let me take, I would lie awake and listen to the trumpeting of the elephants in the San Diego Zoo a couple blocks away, imagining myself a brave explorer in the African jungle.

During that year, I worked construction, attended college, and partied with my friends. I was busy, having fun, and in general being a good citizen. Yet I knew that the cigarette stubs and empty beer cans that littered our coffee table would be a horror for my father to see.

One Sunday morning, after a Saturday night of raucous reveling, I was sleeping in, hungover, when the doorbell rang. I padded to the door in my boxers and opened it. There was Dad, dressed in his out-of-date brown suit, standing on the porch.

"What do you want?" I asked suspiciously, closing the door slightly.

"Can I come in?" He looked uncomfortable. If he'd worn a hat, I'm sure he would have been holding it, running his hands around the rim nervously.

I didn't know what to say. I shook my head but opened the door anyway.

He passed me and walked inside. Before him were the remains of a night of merrymaking: records strewn about, burgeoning ashtrays, empty beer cans, and the stale smell of cigarettes and marijuana lingering in the air.

He sat down on the couch, and I sat opposite him in the beanbag chair. He looked around, surveying the room. I watched his face carefully for signs of judgment. By this time in my life, I was well prepared to argue with him—to attack his lifestyle and to defend mine. I sat there uncomfortably, my mind in high gear, cataloging the persuasive arguments I'd use to battle his puritanical judgments.

But he said nothing—just sat there, looking around, taking it in. Finally, I said testily, "What do you *want*?"

He took a deep breath, and I steeled myself for the first salvo. He looked at me, then away, and said quietly, "I was just going to church and I wondered if you wanted to come along." He looked back at me expectantly.

My mind was too crowded with arguments and tactics to take it in. It took me a few moments to dump out all that stuff in order to understand what he was saying.

"Church?" I asked. "You want me to go to *church*?" I shook my head, mystified.

"Will you come?"

I looked at him sitting there in his lumpy, old-fashioned brown suit and his clunky Knapp pharmacist shoes, and suddenly I knew that his coming here was as hard for him as anything he'd ever done.

I stood, reeling at the revelation. "Sure," I heard myself say, turning toward the bedroom. "Give me a sec."

CHAPTER NINE

Compass

Just ask—there's no telling what you
might get.

In 1943 Dad was nineteen, just out of high school. He'd been drafted into the service and was allowed to choose the army, navy, or marines. He chose the army, asking to be assigned to the air corps, where perhaps he could be an airplane mechanic. Instead, he was assigned to the infantry and soon found himself at Camp Swift, Texas, about ninety miles north of San Antonio, along with thousands of other young men who were being prepared for the impending D-day invasion of Europe.

At Camp Swift, he trained in hand-to-hand combat and the M-1 rifle and spent many cold nights on bivouac, eating C rations.

But as things progressed, and the inevitable loomed ever larger over him, he began to feel blue about his situation. He was a thousand miles from home and didn't have a soul to talk to. Well, maybe one.

So one evening after lights-out he walked out onto the dark parade ground, a huge rolling expanse, and knelt down behind a stand of small, newly planted trees and poured out his heart to God. He asked for a favor: not to get him out of the service altogether—he was proud to serve—but simply to get him transferred to the air corps, where he might use his aptitude for engines and motor repair and serve as a flight mechanic.

In return, he promised God that he would not forget him. And with that simple bargain he stood and walked back to the barracks.

He didn't know the odds against his transfer—he didn't even know how to go about asking for one—but he checked around and wrote a few letters asking for help. He soon discovered that as part of the application he would have to take a physical and pass a written exam. The prospect of a written exam was daunting enough, but passing the physical would be impossible.

Here's why. At age twelve Dad was playing football with some buddies in his front yard, and going out for a pass he ran headlong into a large hedge. He emerged with blood trickling out of his ear. He'd punctured his eardrum.

In those days there was no microsurgery (and very little micro anything), so Dad's eardrum went unrepaired, and he suffered throughout his life with a constant, painful ringing in that damaged ear.

He reported for his physical. He knew he could not pass the hearing test, so instead of covering his good ear as he was supposed to do when they tested his bad one, he kept his hand slightly raised so he could hear something, *anything*.

He passed the test, feeling relieved and slightly guilty, and was preparing to leave when he discovered that the tests he was taking were for the aviation cadets—to learn to fly planes, not just be a mechanic.

Now, to many, if not most, young men, the idea of flying is a romantic and exciting one, as it was for Dad. But he lacked the most rudimentary self-esteem to believe he could ever be a pilot. He'd been a C student in high school, barely graduating. All his life he never thought of himself as smart. So when he sat down to take the aviation cadet exam, his depression outweighed even his great excitement at the prospect of flying.

He plugged through the exam, remembering his pact with God. He knew he must do his part, even if it was hopeless. To cheer himself up, he figured that when—not if—he failed the exam and washed out they might still let him stay in the air corps as a mechanic on the planes he could never hope to fly himself.

When he returned to his unit, the other GIs ridiculed him, saying he'd never get a transfer out of the infantry. It just didn't happen, not at this stage of the war.

But not twenty days later, while out on the firing range, a lieutenant called out to him, "Hey, Kemp, you lucky dog—you hit the jackpot! Your transfer came through."

In later years, Dad said that out of five hundred men in his battalion only he and one other guy even tried to get transferred, and he was the only one who actually succeeded. No one else had even considered trying.

So by the time he was twenty-one, he was a pilot, a commander of a B-24 bomber over the South Pacific. He captained fifteen successful missions, never losing a man, and returned home after the war, where he did his best to keep his end of his promise.

He used to smile and say, "Watch it when you make a bargain with the Lord. Sometimes he goes and fixes it up."

CHAPTER TEN

Plumb Line

It might be hard to always love your
enemies, but you don't have to hate them
either.

Years passed. Dad married, went to college, and started his family. After graduation he moved back to San Diego, where he worked a job as a pharmacist in a small corner drugstore.

After a couple of years he got a job at a new regional hospital and was soon elevated to department head. He also served as chaplain, visiting the sick and dying, encouraging them to have faith and hope. He was well liked and worked hard. I never heard him talk disparagingly about anyone, and neither did I ever hear anyone knock him. He liked people, and they seemed to like him.

But as they say, "There arose up a new Pharaoh, which knew not Joseph." A high-profile administrator was appointed by the hospital board. This new administrator invited Dad into his private office to discuss pharmacy policy.

It was common knowledge around the hospital that Dad was religious and an active member of his church congregation. The administrator asked Dad if that was true. Dad, thinking this a good opportunity to share his faith, nodded. The administrator leaned forward and hissed, "My wife *used* to be a member of your church. I hate you people—you're a bunch of self-righteous prigs. And if it's the last thing I do, I'll have your job."

Dad sat back, stunned. He hesitated a moment, then stood and left without a word. When I heard the story, I was disappointed in my father's reaction. If it had been me, I would have been across that guy's desk in a second with his tie wound around my fist and our eyes inches apart, saying, "Fine. If you want a fight, you got it. But if you come after me, you'd better be ready for nuclear war."

I saw a jerk who needed his ears cuffed, but Dad saw a man whose soul was miserable and small, a man who desperately needed the very things he hated Dad for believing in.

Because of Dad's poor eyesight and bad hearing, his co-workers had always cut him some slack; they knew where his heart was, after all. But the administrator eventually made good on his threat and replaced him with a young, graduate-degree sycophant lackey. Dad was demoted to the pharmacy counter, where he was required to stand on his feet for eight hours at a stretch, trying to hear the customers over the hospital din.

By then Dad was in his late fifties, overweight, and probably clinically depressed. He had to support his large family, so he took it on the chin. He spent much of his time at home in the garage, quietly working on his projects, which didn't plot against him or betray him. He withdrew silently. I never heard him complain.

After more than ten years of this, finally and inevitably, he made a mistake big enough to be formally reprimanded. No one ever suffered because of his mistake; he just "couldn't keep up," according to his dossier. He "lacked relationship skills," it said in another place. And "it was best for all if he would retire," it concluded.

So Dad retired. He never went to war against his aggressor. He simply went about his business, doing the best he could and not giving in to hate or anger.

At the time I thought he was really just afraid to fight.

CHAPTER ELEVEN

Power

Everything has more than one purpose—
including people.

After Dad retired, he and Mom decided they would like to volunteer as missionaries for their church for a couple of years. They were assigned to Guatemala. The prospect of learning Spanish at their age was daunting, but they were excited to go to such an exotic place and were eager to share their faith.

Life often throws a mean curveball. The day after they received their assignment, Dad was informed by his doctor during a routine medical examination that he had amyotrophic lateral sclerosis (ALS), commonly known as Lou Gehrig's disease, an incurable, fatal illness. ALS results in slow, creeping paralysis in which the brain sends the muscles signals they do not hear. The victim is slowly paralyzed from the extremities inward, while the mind remains clear. There is no blessed dementia as with Alzheimer's. Your body simply dies around you, and you have total awareness of what is happening yet no power whatsoever to prevent it.

We couldn't believe it. No one in our family had ever faced anything like this. We thought it must be a mistake or at the very least a trial sent by God that our faith would overcome. So Mom and Dad accepted their assignment and left for Guatemala, hoping and praying for the best.

In Central America, Dad instantly felt a deep compassion and warmth for the Guatemalan people. He admired their openness and humility as well as their ability to make do with so little. On their days off, he and Mom toured the archaeological sites he had read about for so many years. They visited market-places and tried to speak with people in their frac-tured Spanish. But after a few months, Dad's condi-tion deteriorated to the extent that he could not walk without assistance. Because he would not allow him-self to become a burden on others, they sadly returned to the States.

My father believed in a God who knows each of us by name. Once back home, however, he was perplexed that his prayers were apparently going unanswered. He couldn't understand why God wouldn't heal him, at least for the period of time he was trying to bring faith and hope to people who so desperately needed it. He knew he had been faithful and had worked hard, but the diagnosis remained: he had no more than eighteen months to live.

The truth is that ALS seemed eerily tailor-made to test Dad's notorious self-sufficiency. He was the guy you'd most like to have around in a worst-case scenario because he would find a way through it. When it comes to building things, I've always said that if you gave Dad the raw materials, he could build you a nuclear bomb. Apparently, there wasn't anything he could not rethink, repair, reuse, or recycle.

ALS was a problem no wrench or nail could solve, and underneath his stoic exterior I sensed a growing desperation. Once, when we were discussing the prognosis, I thought I saw fear in his eyes, and I had a revelation: he was going to die. It startled me. I hadn't believed it right up until that very moment.

Dad beat back his fear and the urge to quit. Instead, he rolled up his sleeves and set to work. He studied his disease in earnest, hoping there was a little-known treatment that might help. He also studied the scriptures, trying to glean an understanding of why his life had taken this turn. Most of all he prayed fervently, asking for peace of mind and the ability to accept his fate, if that was God's will.

When the doctors noticed his extremely high white blood cell count, Dad consented to chemotherapy. And although the white cell count was reduced and the progress of the disease was slowed, ALS maintained its inexorable march forward. Now, instead of having eighteen months, he had three years of creeping paralysis to suffer through before the end.

Through his medical studies he became more of an ALS expert than his doctors, whose practices involve helping patients prepare for death. Most of Dr. Kervorkian's "patients" are ALS sufferers. Dad said once that although he could empathize with their desire to end their lives, that road was not for him. I was amazed at his strength and courage and suddenly realized that my father was not afraid of a fight after all; he just didn't bother with the minor skirmishes.

At the same time, a prominent church leader's advanced lymphoma suddenly went into remission. At a family gathering, someone commented how wonderful it was that God had answered the prayers of so many in healing this man. We all looked at Dad to see his reaction. He said simply, "I guess I'm not as important as he is." Everyone protested, but later, when we were alone, Dad asked me what I thought.

I looked at him, sitting heavily in his lounger, his hands nearly useless at his sides, his hair thin from the chemotherapy, but his eyes bright and expressive.

"Maybe he *is* more important than you," I said quietly. "Or maybe he still has something important left to do on this earth. And maybe you've accomplished everything you were supposed to do here. Maybe your time is up."

Dad nodded. "Maybe you're right," he said and looked away.

My father was no talker. His punctured eardrum with its constant ringing, combined with the cacophony of family life with seven kids, often left him irritable and headachy. When we would engage in heated debates around the dinner table, he would excuse himself and go out to the garage where it was quiet. Ironically, with ALS destroying his body, all that was left him now was speech, and even that was fading. He had always been a physical man, handling greasy car parts, hefting a ten-pound sledge, kicking my bed to wake me on Saturday mornings. Now, with his body closing down, he looked at me, his eyes full of emotion, his mouth working, but the words slurred and hard to understand.

He once said to me, "I never felt like anyone special. I don't have any real talents, and I'm slow and clumsy. So who am I to be noticed by anybody—especially by God?

"But if God never noticed me before, I'm pretty

sure he's watching me now, to see how I'll handle this. So maybe *this* is my moment of truth. And if it is, I'd sure hate to disappoint him by being a coward."

He smiled at me in his crooked, squinty way.

I shook my head in wonder. I wasn't sure whether God was watching him or not, but I *was* sure of one thing: he was no coward.

CHAPTER TWELVE

Chisel

Ask good questions—then be sure to
listen.

I read somewhere that there are only two B-24 Liberators still flying in the United States. One is a mail plane in Alaska, and the other makes the rounds to air shows. Dad called me up and asked me to take him down to Lindbergh Field to see this last Liberator before he died. It took a moment to register. I couldn't believe he'd said it that bluntly: before he *died*. I swallowed hard. "Come on, Dad," I said tentatively, "you're gonna be around for a long time yet."

"Maybe," he said. "But the plane might not be. They were always falling out of the sky for no reason."

I laughed. He continued, "You know why they call it pilot *error*, don't you?"

"No."

"Because you just get one."

❖ ◆ ❖

We arrived at the airport on a warm, muggy spring morning. Dad wore his pilot's cap and his aging leather flight jacket. He was confined to a wheelchair, and I pushed him slowly across the tarmac, toward the rusty, olive green bomber.

"There she is," he said proudly, like he had flown her himself.

I stopped pushing and stared. *This* was the famous plane I'd heard so much about, the one both Dad and I had built models of? *This* unimpressive, precariously small thing?

"She's a beauty, isn't she?"

She was not. She was hardly bigger than a Lear jet and looked held together by baling wire. I rolled Dad up to her and helped him to his feet. I steadied him as he reached up and gingerly touched the peeling paint, like it was a holy relic.

"Set me down," he said, smiling as wide as I ever remember. "Now, you be me. Get up there in the cockpit and tell me what you see."

I crawled into the plane. There was no insulation, nothing to cover the bare wires, cables, or exposed frame. I squeezed through a small hole in the cockpit floor. Even if Dad wasn't sick, it's unlikely he'd have been able to get through the tiny manhole. I was glad he was spared that indignity.

I sat in the cracked webbed pilot seat and scanned the control panel, such as it was. There were only about ten small gauges, compared with dozens in today's planes. I had flown scores of hours with Dad at the wheel and never felt even a twinge of fear. However, sitting here in this rattletrap, a plane thrown together to be thrown aloft, I was struck by a sudden, overpowering fear. This thing could not possibly fly. It was too poorly designed, too cobbled together, too dangerous. Imagine flying this plane with a full bomb bay—maybe at night—while you were being shot at. It would be like flying a stick of TNT. I shuddered.

"How is it?" I heard Dad ask cheerfully.

I craned my neck out the window. "It's amazing," I said honestly. "You must have been nuts—you really flew these?"

Dad was still grinning. "Yeah. And over water, too!"

Right. Don't forget to worry about the water. As I clambered out of the plane I wondered if storming Normandy Beach would have been safer than going up in one of these.

Months passed. One day I arrived for a visit. As I walked through the garage, I noticed that the work-bench was dusty. It struck me that Dad hadn't been out here in over a year. I went inside and was shocked at his deterioration. He sat listlessly in his easy chair, unable to hold a book to read or even to concentrate on television. Strangely, he had lost little weight. He was still substantial, but the heaviness in his muscles was not vibrant; it was becoming deadweight.

One eerie characteristic of the disease is the way the brain's messages are garbled. Individual muscle groups in Dad's legs and forearms continually jumped and twitched, as if they were reacting to constant shocks. In the early stages of the disease, we would watch this strange dance and shake our heads in disbelief, trying to imagine how it must feel to watch your own body go out of control.

This time as I entered I noticed that the muscle twitches that had so long been a visual reminder of the disease had vanished. Dad was pale, and his breathing was shallow. His arms and legs lay motionless. Mom sat by him, feeding him something that didn't require much chewing. His eyes brightened when he saw me, and he immediately burst into tears.

The effect was so alarming and disarming that I found myself crying as well. I knelt down by his side and squeezed his hand. His grip was weak and his hand cool. His body was shutting down, and only the radiance in his tearful eyes indicated the fire in his heart.

CHAPTER THIRTEEN

Blade

Every job worth starting is worth finishing.

On August 16, 1990, my sister Bonnie called to tell me that Dad's time was short. I hurried down Interstate 5 and arrived in La Mesa at 11 A.M. He had been placed in a hospital bed in the living room under the lunar landing module chandelier. It was hard to look at him. His breathing was labored, his skin was cold, and his eyes had lost their luster. He was close to the end. Unable to swallow, he hadn't eaten anything in several days. My sister Bonnie rubbed ice over his parched lips.

I sat down on the bed and held one hand as Mom held the other. I spoke softly, trying to give him strength as he faced the darkness. His eyes began to glaze over, and his breathing was shallow and intermittent. He was visibly receding from us. We hugged him. We tried to be strong and hold back the tears. We wanted somehow to ease his suffering, but we knew we could not be with him where he was now.

During the last fifteen minutes, he breathed just once a minute. It seemed like all life had passed from him, and we would exchange devastated looks; then he would gasp for another breath, startling us. This was worse than anything I could have imagined. After several of these episodes, we just wanted the misery to end, to see him released from the bondage of a body that so cruelly imprisoned him.

Finally, he seemed to relax, and the light went out of his hazy eyes. I looked down and knew, in that instant, that I was no longer holding my father's hand. I had an image of him, suddenly a million light-years away, in the arms of his own father. Mom, Bonnie, and I exchanged looks of sad relief. Mom began to cry quietly. Then she looked up, wiped her tears away, and said, brightening, "You know what? He can finally hear in *both* ears!"

We laughed and cried at the same time.

CHAPTER FOURTEEN

Clamp

The answer is always in the most obvious place.

According to our religious tradition, the night before the funeral our family gathered to dress and groom Dad's body for burial. At the mortuary, we entered a darkened room where his body lay on a table under a drape of white linen. A sense of the sacred surrounded us. We spoke quietly. As we moved his body to dress him, I noticed the markings a lifetime of work had given him, familiar scars on his freckled skin. I touched the faint white lines and was reminded of the times he had cut himself or banged his thumb while repairing or building something. Buttoning the white dress shirt over his barrel chest, I recalled his intimidating presence as he stood over me, commanding me to perform a chore. As I glanced at my siblings and mother, I knew they were all feeling the same thing. Someone said that it was strange—although this *looked* like Dad, it wasn't him, really. It was just a body, and he was far, far away. Everyone nodded. I hoped it was true.

The next day at the funeral, I listened intently to the music and eulogies, but the profound weight of the moment seemed to glance off me, narrowly missing my heart. I expected to be overwhelmed with grief. I had been there when he died; I had experienced that tragic moment. With his body in the casket at the front of the chapel, I expected the loss and sadness to engulf me. It didn't. The emotions were there, but I was strangely disconnected from them. Then I thought, *Maybe I have more faith than I knew. Perhaps not even the death of my father can put a dent in it.* But that wasn't true. I didn't feel faithful. And then an assassin idea came unbidden, the most criminal thought ever: *Maybe I don't feel anything because there is nothing to feel. Maybe I never really loved him at all.*

For a long time afterward I was depressed and confused. I wondered what was wrong with me.

CHAPTER FIFTEEN

Chalk Line

There is a tool for every job. Keep yours handy.

Finally I began to feel a little better, and I shifted my attention from myself to Mom. I began to watch her for signs of healing grief. She said she cried when she was alone, but she wasn't tearful around me. As she threw herself into a flurry of church and family activity, I thought maybe she was still in denial. I figured she really *was* feeling the loss but didn't want to show a lack of faith. I imagined her telling herself, *What do you have to be sad about? Don't you believe you'll see him again?* I wondered how she'd answer that.

To make matters worse, once Dad was gone, Mom didn't change a thing beyond removing his sickbed from the living room. Everything else remained as before. His clothing hung in his closet; dresser drawers still held his belongings. I was afraid for her in that lonely, empty house, which was so full of Dad's industry. He was in every piece of paneling, furniture, and molding. I wondered how much it hurt her to see the one she had loved so much everywhere she looked.

It occurred to me that I might be able to help her past the denial stage by making small changes to her environment. Doing anything inside the house was out of the question; she'd never permit it. I figured the garage would be the perfect place. She rarely went out there anyway. Once I cleaned it out, she would discover she had survived and would see that Dad was not really in the things he'd collected. I hoped she'd see that her surroundings didn't need to remain unchanged for him to still be kept safely in her heart. I didn't want Mom to forget Dad, but I saw her retreating into loneliness and despair. I called my brother Virl and told him my plan.

He said he'd be glad to help.

CHAPTER SIXTEEN

Nails

The act of straightening nails is more
important than the result.

So on the day before Christmas I stood looking at the painting of the Tetons on the garage door, thinking about my dad and waiting for my brother to arrive. When he finally did, I raised the garage door and we surveyed the area, knowing it would take more than one trip to the dump to clean out a garage that Dad spent forty years filling up. Carpet that had been replaced in the house had never made it past the garage floor. I guess Dad thought his cars deserved deep plush underfoot, too.

Workbench drawers groaned with their heavy burdens—a deep drawer for wrenches, another for screwdrivers, one for sockets, one for wire, another for switches, another for all manner of electrical doodads and gizmos that had meaning only for Dad.

Overhead hung two dozen glass Miracle Whip jars, their lids screwed to the low ceiling, their insides full of every kind of screw, bolt, washer, and nail. I unscrewed one and examined it. I was amazed that, in my entire life, I saw only one of those heavy quart jars fall. It was luck, I guess, but the long lag screws securing the lids to the ceiling must have helped, too.

I dumped the contents onto the workbench: a fist-sized jumble of straightened eightpenny galvanized nails. I recalled all the Saturdays I had spent pounding those bent nails straight again, only to go with Dad to the lumberyard where he would buy brand-new ones, while my refurbished nails languished, unused. It wasn't until I was an adult that I understood the purpose of the nail-straightening ritual.

Virl backed the trailer into the driveway, and we got to work. We hauled out armfuls of scrap wood, aluminum electrical conduit, old iron bars, and appliance motors of every description. Around our house, the only part of an obsolete washing machine that ever made it to the curb was the metal shell. Everything else was kept for future use.

When Dad built a living room addition and moved the front door to the true front of the house, he raised the entryway to the same level, which resulted in a long hallway with a three-foot-high crawl space underneath—a perfect place to store almost anything you would probably never need again but wanted to keep anyway. I reached behind the water heater, opened the access door, and switched on the light Dad had rigged in there. The crawl space was full. I shook my head wearily. "I'm not cleaning that out. No way," I said, closing the door.

Virl nodded. "Let the next owners worry about it." (If you ever need a motor for a 1964 Kenmore washing machine, it's in there. Help yourself.)

We hauled out broken screen doors, every shape and size of wood, aluminum metal flanges, and rusty cans of thirty-year-old paint. The paint cans struck me oddly. Most of them were so old the paint didn't even slosh anymore. It was perplexing, all this paint. Why did he keep it? Dad hated painting so much he'd just panel the wall instead. So of course every room in Mom's house is wood grained.

Occasionally we found objects that virtually shouted Dad's name. We found a series of nameplates from the grilles of all the cars he had ever owned: the '53 Oldsmobile sedan, the green Dodge Sierra I wrecked; the stylish maroon Ford LTD; the unforgettable chocolate brown Chrysler Imperial with fins so large we called it the Batmobile.

We even found several painted ceramic mermaid figurines Grandpa had given to Dad. They were vaguely risqué, and Virl and I laughed. Dad was so proper, he never hung them up in plain view but stored them secretly in a deep drawer. We put them back. They must have had some sort of meaning for him. We would respect that sentiment.

I hauled a dusty olive green ammo box out from under the workbench. It looked familiar. I opened it, and stale air that had been trapped for years arose, smelling of old rubber. Inside I found a yellowed rubber bag with Dad's childhood marble collection inside: bright green and yellow cat's-eyes; silver steelies; large, pitted black shooters. Dad had played with these marbles when he was a kid, and I played with the same marbles when I was young, although I never really learned the art of it. The rubbery smell of the bag transported me back thirty years to a hot summer sidewalk, me squatting on my haunches, a marble held tightly in my hand, concentrating on the trajectory.

Virl opened the tool drawers. Dad was like Noah: he'd collected two of every kind. He was happiest in two places in this world: in the cockpit of an airplane or walking the aisles of a hardware store. I am not a pilot, but I have inherited his love for hardware stores and can wander the aisles, drinking in the intoxicating smells and marveling at the inventiveness of a new kind of wrench until my legs give out and I return home, drained yet strangely refreshed.

In the spaces between the overhead beams, Dad crammed lengths of wood, aluminum siding, electrical conduit, and anything else that wouldn't fit in a drawer. I reached up and began pulling things out, marveling at how every nook and cranny was filled. Then I pulled out a piece of three-quarter-inch exterior-quality plywood, four inches wide and eighteen inches long, painted a bright, light bluish green. I'd seen it before, but I couldn't remember where. I stared at the wood, turning it over in my hands, my ears buzzing.

Suddenly I knew why I was there in Dad's garage the day before Christmas. *That* green piece of plywood was why.

It was a talisman.

CHAPTER SEVENTEEN

Plane

Family vacations are mandatory—theme parks are not.

In 1962, when I was seven, Dad took the whole family to the Seattle World's Fair. Our Dodge Sierra station wagon was new then, a shiny two-tone green with modest fins and Naugahyde bench seats.

Because there were eight of us (my youngest sister had not yet been born), we couldn't afford to stay in motels. Like always, Dad had a plan. He built a plywood box nearly as large as the car roof and two feet deep. He painted it to match the car, then secured it to the rooftop like an oversized luggage rack. The box had a lid that could be removed and slipped inside the car over the tops of the bench seats, upon which he and Mom slept. My brother and I slept in the box on top of the car, and my sisters slept snugly inside the car on the seats beneath the lid. We camped out in that style all the way to Seattle.

During our drive north I sat in the rear-facing backseat with my younger sister Cheryl. In between reading my stack of science fiction novels (I remember in particular Isaac Asimov's *I, Robot*), knitting a wallet (yes, my mother taught me to knit, thank you very much), singing songs, and occasionally fighting with Cheryl, I would wave so persistently to people following us that they would pass just to avoid having to wave back at me for the hundredth time.

We toured the sequoia forests of northern California, drove through a tunnel cut through the base of a giant redwood tree, climbed on every statue we found, and gawked up at a humongous cement Paul Bunyan and his blue ox, Babe. To this day I still remember the acrid, musty smell of the Crown-Zellerbach paper factory on the Columbia River in Oregon.

When we returned from our trip, Dad converted the travel box into a bunk bed for my brother and me. The box became the lower bunk where Virl slept. I slept in the upper bunk, which was made from the lid.

When my brother went to college a few years

later, Dad took the bed apart and made Virl's bunk into a large eight-drawer dresser, which my sisters used for many years. The lid made its way to the garage and served as the foundation for my model HO gauge railroad set. It was attached to the ceiling with ropes and pulleys, and I could lower it, setting it on two sawhorses, when I wanted to play trains.

Five years later, the train was long forgotten, but the dresser remained and stood in my room. It was the year before I left for college. I had ceased connecting the dresser with the travel box because by then it had been painted a dark brown. The dresser still stands in one of Mom's guest bedrooms.

As I stood there in the garage, I remembered that piece of plywood through all its evolutions, from the moment Dad picked it out at the lumberyard until the moment I found myself holding the last slice of it, thirty years later.

As I felt its substance, it began to dawn on me: Dad really *was* gone, and with him his ability to see something new and useful inside something old and worn. To him, a piece of plywood wasn't just lumber: it was a travel box, a bunk bed, a train set platform, or a dresser.

I had shared most of my life with this piece of plywood as shaped by my father's hand. It had joined me on an unforgettable family vacation. I had worn the paint off the ladder climbing up to sleep in a bed made from it. I had played trains on it. I had placed my clothing in its drawers. Now at last I held a remnant of it, the craftsman's busy hand finally still and the wood at rest, no longer to be cut and nailed, sanded, and painted.

A thunderous wave of loss came rushing forward, burying me. I staggered under its weight. I sobbed, unaware of anyone else, my grief finally loosened. My mind moved ahead to an empty future: my unborn children would never know him, never see his squinty smile or watch him measure and plan, saw and nail. I would never again hand him a wrench and wonder how he was going to fix *this* bit of mechanical trouble.

CHAPTER EIGHTEEN

Hammer

Be a carpenter. Build something
worthwhile. Start with yourself.

During the time we spent cleaning the garage, Mom came out only once and then quickly went back inside. I glanced over at the piece of green plywood on the workbench and finally understood. I felt foolish about my pop psychology "stages of grief" notions. In her own way, Mom was grieving already, coping the best way she knew how—privately and silently. How could she not grieve? Dad's imprint, smell, and essence surrounded her wherever she went in that house and every day reminded her of his absence.

Perhaps her grieving began the day he died and she went into their bedroom to get something and opened his closet and saw his pilot's hat sitting on the shelf. Maybe it was the next day when she entered the den and saw dozens of his airplane photos on the wall. Or perhaps she even began to grieve two months before he passed away, as she crawled alone into the bed they'd shared for forty years after kissing him goodnight as he lay in a cold hospital bed in the living room.

For me the grieving began four months after he died, on the day before Christmas, in the cluttered garage where I had grown up under my father's watchful and stern eye, surrounded by the materials with which he had built his life and mine.

I stood holding a simple piece of green plywood, a silent but eloquent witness of the greatness of a man who never knew he was.

Perhaps he was a carpenter after all.

O. C. Kemp